# The Itty Bitty Kitty Committee

# The Itty Bitty Kitty Committee

Laurie Cinotto

ROARING BROOK PRESS

NEW YORK

For my sweetest supporters:
the kitten who perched on my shoulder,
the cat who napped on my desk,
and the husband who stood by my side.

Roaring Brook Press books may be purchased for business or promotional use. For information on bulk purchases please contact Macmillan Corporate and Premium Sales Department at (800) 221-7945 x5442 or by e-mail at specialmarkets@macmillan.com.

First edition 2014
Book design by Roberta Pressel
Printed in China by Toppan
Leefung Printing Ltd.,
Dongguan City, Guangdong
Province
10 9 8 7 6 5
4 3 2 1

Library of Congress Cataloging-in-Publication Data
Cinotto, Laurie.
    The Itty Bitty Kitty Committee / Laurie Cinotto.— First edition.
       pages cm
    Summary: "A hip, fun, photo-heavy guide to all things kitten from the eponymous website"—Provided by publisher.
    ISBN 978-1-59643-937-5 (paperback)
1. Kittens—Juvenile literature. 2. Kittens—Pictorial works—Juvenile literature. 3. Itty Bitty Kitty Committee—Juvenile literature. 4. Foster care of animals—Juvenile literature. 5. Cat adoption—Juvenile literature. I. Title.

SF445.7.C56 2014
636.8'07—dc23

2013023155

# Contents

# An Itty Bitty Introduction

**My name is Laurie, and I am a kitten wrangler.**

When young kittens are surrendered to animal shelters, there isn't always enough space to house them or staff to care for them. Kittens are needy in this early stage of life, so they are sent into foster homes where they can be closely monitored and raised by volunteers until they reach an adoptable age.

My husband, Craig, and I are foster parents, or "kitten wranglers." We were introduced to the Humane Society for Tacoma and Pierce County's foster program when we adopted a fostered kitten, Charlene Butterbean. When Charlene was about a year old, we took in our first litter and tried fostering too. That was six years and nearly 200 kittens ago!

Sometimes kittens come to us healthy, sometimes they're sick. Sometimes they are scared of humans and we have to teach them to trust, sometimes they start purring the second they step into our home and climb into our laps. Each batch is different, but by the time they are ready to be adopted and leave our home, they're happy, healthy, loving, and confident kittens.

I started my blog, The Itty Bitty Kitty Committee, to share stories and photos of our kittens so families could get to know them, fall in love, and adopt these precious babes. I also wanted to use the blog to share the fostering/kitten wrangling experience with others in the hope of encouraging them to give it a try too.

Meeting these tiny kittens is a privilege, and watching them grow and flourish is a wonderful sight to behold. I feel so lucky to live a life that allows me to foster and witness their growth each day. Of course there are messes to clean up, many litter boxes to scoop, a few worries along the way, and all those good-byes we have to say, but the joy these kittens bring us while they're in our care outweighs any of the hard parts!

I'm excited to show you our Itty Bitty world in the pages ahead, to introduce you to some of our kittens, to tell you a few kitten tales, and to share a few kitten-raising lessons we've learned along the way. We've had the pleasure of meeting many fabulous kittens, and I think you're going to enjoy meeting them too!

*Laurie Cinotto*

**Lead Kitten Wrangler**
**The Itty Bitty Kitty Committee**

# All the Itty Bitty Kitties

**THE ORIGINAL IBKC**
Penny, Cassius, Vinnie, and Pierre

**THE HOPPS/VONTROUTS**
Wendell Jefferson Hopps, Mitzy Jean Hopps,
Reva VonTrout, Rex VonTrout

**THE BOUVIERS**
Cornelius, Lottie, Maddie,
and Willamena

**THE MAYFIELDS**
(FROM TOP TO BOTTOM)
Fergus, Auggie, Porter, Clementine,
and Leroy

Bernadette Mayfield

**THE PICKETTS**
(FROM TOP TO BOTTOM)
Twyla, Ruth Anne, Jerry Lee, Lovell, and Nadine

**THE PETTIBONES**
Alvie, Carmine, Rosalie, Virgil, Renata,
and Agnes

**THE DAVENPORTS**
Edward and Cecily, Chet, Inez, and Orson

### THE LIVERMORE FOUR
Lyle, Trudy, Albert, and Davy

### THE LOVEJOYS
Tressa, Neville, Harlan, and Nelson

### THE LABATH LADIES
Hester Sue, Enid, Georgette, and Miranda

### THE ASHBYS
Milton, Clovis, Rupert, Norman, and Josephine "Bunny"

### THE DARLING DARLINGS
Lucinda, Hubert "Hubie," Francine, Rhoda, and Selma

### THE FORTUNATO FIVE
Philippa "Pippy" Allegra, Gaetano, Warren, Luigi, and Dominick

### THE MUSSELMANS
Olly, Arthur, Darla, and Benny

### THE DRAPERS
Luella, Gordon, Millicent "Millie," and Perry

### THE FINCH BOYS
Ira and Walter

### THE SPOONERS
Vivienne and Theodore

### THE LYTTELTONS
Ridley, Ezra, Gia, Thelma, Fern, and Pia

## THE ANDERSON-ERICKSONS
Louise, Bernice, Ambrose, Ferris, Emory, and Clement

## THE SUPRENANT SISTERS
Biscuit, Camille, Betty June, Marie-Noir, and Ve Ching

## THE FURMAN FIVE
Teddy, Curtis, Edith, Oliver, and Roland

## THE LIVELY BUNCH
Truman, Lambert O, Irving, and Fiona

## THE FROSTS
Nigel and Mimsey

## THE BARTLETTS
Imogene, Georgie, Marcel, and Clarence

## THE MEDLEYS
Linus, Beezus, Maxine, Peter, Freddie Jean, and Kirby Nesbitt

## THE EASTERBROOKS
Astrid, Thurston, and Norma

## THE DEARBORNS
Geraldine, Pearla, Phoebe, Marla, and Sheldon

## THE BATSELS
Clifford, Barnum, Claudius Felix, and Priscilla

## THE MCGILLICUDDY GIRLS
Victoria Anne, Cheryl, and Opal

## THE WIGGINS
Susanna Rose, Kenneth, Tilda, Buster

## THE TRIMBLE TABBY TRIO
Monroe, Bess, and Wee Willard

## THE KNAPPS
Cecil, Sylvie, and Wylie

## THE LAMMS
Edison, Baxter, Zelda, and Edna

## THE WINKLERS
Flip, Franklin, Bibi, Leonard, and Daphne

## THE GIBSONS
Charles Laurent, Pheona, Sherman, Cedric, and Rutherford "Ruddy"

## THE PETRIES
Pearl Mae, Sir Reginald, Aloysius Rosebud, and Forrest

## THE SMALLS
Violet, Solomon "Sol," Louie "Shrimp Louie," and Liam

## THE LOUDERMILKS
Cyrus, Clive, Ralphie, and Graham

## THE TIPTON TABBIES
Royal, Jimmy, and Floyd

## THE STOUTS
Audrey, Filbert, and Wylla

**W**hen choosing names for kittens, we select a last name that reflects a personality or physical trait of the litter. With the Lamms, it was both. They were sweet gentle lambs, and they had woolly lamblike coats too.

There were four in this litter—three were varieties of Siamese, and one was an orange tabby boy named Baxter.

In the world of kittens, an orange tabby is more common than a Siamese, but in this bunch, Baxter was the unusual one.

Baxter

Edna and Edison were Lynx Point Siamese, the woollier ones of the bunch, and nearly identical. The easiest way to tell them apart was that Edison could often be found wriggling around, belly side up. Edna was much more dignified than that, and she preferred not to share her tummy with the world.

Edison & Edna

Zelda

Zelda was a very spirited Seal Point, and the tiniest of the flock. What she lacked in size, she made up for in determination.

The best part about the Lamms was how much they loved each other. They were a close-knit group, always playing in a pack or napping in a huddle.

They would fall into the most impossibly adorable positions while they slept. Watching them nap was even more entertaining than watching them play!

# Bringing Home Baby

Before the kitten comes home, be prepared with the following supplies:

- Cat carrier
- Kitty litter
- Litter scoop
- Scratching post
- Water dish
- Dry food
- Bed
- Litter box
- Toys
- Food dish
- Wet food

- Bringing home a new kitten is exciting for the humans in your household, but it can be a little stressful for the kitty. There are many changes for the kitten to adjust to, so it's important to do everything you can to make this transition easy.

- Start by creating a safe, cozy space for kitty—an extra bedroom, bathroom, laundry room, or any small, enclosed space will work. Set up the food, water, litter box, and a comfy bed. Provide plenty of toys.

- Let kitty spend a few days here and get used to the sounds and smells of his new home.

- He may be frightened and want to hide. Be quiet, patient, and gentle, and help him feel calm and safe.

- If he retreats, approach him slowly and encourage him to come out from hiding by offering some food or a toy.

- When he seems comfortable, let him begin exploring the rest of his new world, and then you can slowly start the process of introducing him to the other animals in the house.

- These introductions can be stressful for your other animals; you never quite know how they'll react. Some will get along from the start, but for others it may take weeks for the bonding process to start. Always make sure an adult handles these introductions.

# KITTY COMICS

## Plotting Pettibones

Ok, here's the plan.
Alvie, when the door opens, run over and distract her by rolling over on your back. Show her your belly stripes, start purring and making air biscuits. That gets her every time.

Now, Virgil, wait a couple of seconds, go sit on the rug, and start making noises like you're going to throw up.

When she runs over to help you, I will make a run for the kitchen. I know there's tuna in there, I could smell it this morning. I promise to eat enough for all three of us. Are you ready? Here she comes. . . .

Playful
Kittens

# Playtime

**Play is an important part of a kitten's development.** It stimulates his mind, gives him exercise, and it's a way for you to bond with your new kitty. Devote plenty of time to play and interact with your kitty each day. The more time you spend together, the less time he has to get bored and find trouble!

• **Have a variety of toys on hand.** Kittens like balls to chase, toys that crinkle, feather wands to leap after, soft toys to wrestle with, and hard toys they can chew on.

• **Cat toys don't need to be purchased in a store.** There are plenty of things around the house that can entertain a kitten—like a paper or foil ball, the cardboard core of a paper towel or toilet paper roll, the ring from a plastic milk jug, a paper grocery sack with the handles removed, a large plastic straw, a spool (without thread), or a lid from a plastic bottle.

• **Boxes and laundry baskets are fun to play inside of and make excellent forts!**

• **Play it safe!** If your kitty is trying to bite or scratch, or is playing too rough, give him a toy to wrestle with, and move your hands and feet away from his reach. It's important not to encourage this behavior. It may seem cute now, but if a kitten continues this behavior into adulthood, he could become dangerous.

• **It's easy for a curious kitten to find objects around the house that are dangerous to play with.** Keep things like yarn, string, thread, ribbons, rubber bands, hair ties, earbuds, cords and wires, pins, and plastic bags away from kitty's reach. All of these can cause harm to a kitty if swallowed.

## Charlene Butterbean

**W**hen **Charlene Butterbean** was just a wee thing, only a few days old, she was surrendered to the shelter along with her brother. We don't know who their mama was, if they had a family of humans to care for them, or if they were found in the wild.

After an examination by the vet staff and a little paperwork, the two kitties were placed in a foster home just a few blocks away from our house.

We had just moved into the neighborhood, and I went with a friend to meet our neighbors, Kim and Sarah. Charlene and her twin brother were in their care.

I had never seen such tiny kittens before. They were barely ten days old and their eyes had just opened. They were frail and sickly little things and scarcely had the strength to hold their tiny bodies upright. Their ears pointed to the side, which is normal for a kitten at this stage of development, but it seemed that if they were a little healthier, those ears might point a little bit higher.

The kittens were bottle-fed a special milk made for kittens. They were kept warm and safe and closely watched. Sadly, even with all the love and special care they received, Charlene's little brother passed away. Charlene, who was the healthier of the two from the start, grew and thrived, thanks to the good care she received from Kim and Sarah.

Until I met Charlene, the thought of adding another cat or kitten to our home never entered my mind. We were completely happy with our sweet senior cat, Drewey, a beautiful gray and white tabby girl with a pale pink nose, who had been with us for nearly fourteen years.

But that sweet little puff of a kitten, so awkward and adorable, won our hearts, and we soon decided that she should be ours. We waited patiently for her to grow big enough to be adopted.

Charlene spent her first few weeks of life at Kim and Sarah's house, surrounded by a handful of foster kittens, five adult cats, chinchillas, bunnies, and an occasional visit from a big yellow lab. I think this exposure to so many critters helped prepare her for her life ahead—a parade of kittens.

The day we brought our very first batch of foster kittens home, Charlene was quite curious and immediately attempted to stick her nose inside the bin that contained them.

They were tucked inside a quiet room, and Charlene camped outside the door, hoping to catch another peek. This continued for the next two weeks while we waited for the quarantine period to end. After we knew the kittens were healthy, and it was safe for Charlene to meet them, we let them all mingle.

Charlene immediately took on the role of foster mom and bathed these babies as if they were her own. She's never been a mother; it just came naturally to Charlene.

Now, she's an important part of the fostering process. She nurtures and plays with the kittens. She teaches them boundaries and shows them how to behave around a big cat by giving them love. But she also gives them a firm paw if they get out of line.

They learn to respect her, which is a great preparation for their life ahead—since so many kittens move into homes with adult cats.

## SHE NURTURES AND PLAYS WITH THE KITTENS.

Charlene is a special one. I know not every cat would be so accepting and tolerant of the steady parade of kittens that streams through our home. We feel so lucky to have found her—she was our introduction to the world of fostering, so without her, there would be no Itty Bitty Kitty Committee!

# Game Over

Enid and Miranda LaBath were having a really great time wrestling in and on the paper bag, until Miss Butterbean came along and planted herself right on top of their fun. Game over.

Napping Kittens

# Cat Nap Facts

Kittens play hard and grow fast, and they need lots of rest.
They can sleep up to sixteen hours a day!

• **Kittens and cats don't sleep for long periods of time like humans do**—they take naps of varied lengths throughout the day and night.

• **Kittens sleep more when their owners are away than they do while they're home.**

• **Kittens dream!** We don't know what they're dreaming about, but if you hear a kitty mew in his sleep, or see him twitch his paws, most likely he's dreaming.

• **They follow the sun!** Every kitten and cat enjoys a nap in the warmth of the sun, and they will often move from room to room to stay in a sunlight patch.

# Nigel and Mimsey Frost

**M**y parents, who were visiting us from Iowa, spent a little time with a charming pair of kittens named Walter and Ira Finch. They had met plenty of other litters before, and enjoyed each one, but there was just something special about Walter and Ira. If the timing had been better, my mom would have left with the pair tucked under her arm.

Long after they returned home, my mom kept thinking about those kittens. If they came up in conversation, with a lump in her throat, she would express her regrets for not figuring out how to make them hers.

A year later, **Nigel and Mimsey Frost** moved in with us. I posted their pictures on the blog, and Mom called to tell me she wanted to adopt this pair. Mimsey resembled Walter, and that's what got my mom's attention at first, but it was Nigel's floof that sealed the deal. They were adorable, and Mom couldn't miss out on the opportunity to adopt them.

But how would we get them to Iowa, which is two thousand miles away?

Our friend Kim worked for an airline and commuted to Chicago several times a month. I gave her a call to find out if she might be able to help us get the kittens to the Midwest. She happily agreed and figured out all the necessary steps we needed to take to get the babies on board.

The adoption paperwork was mailed to Iowa to be completed, a special carrier designed for airline travel was purchased, and we decided on a delivery date.

The next few weeks, while we waited for the kittens to grow big enough to be adopted, were filled with many phone calls and e-mail exchanges. These would be my parents' very first kittens, and my mom had a lot of questions.

"What do they eat? How much will they sleep? What do kittens smell like?"

They bought all the needed supplies and prepared the house. They moved plants and knickknacks out of a kitten's reach. They were as ready as they could possibly be.

And, finally, the kittens were ready to go.

We drove to the airport bright and early one Saturday morning. We parked, and I walked with Kim and the kittens up to Security. We said our good-byes, and I watched as they passed through screening. Kim had to pull them out of the carrier and hold one kitten under each arm as she walked though the metal detectors. I was too far away to hear the conversations, but I could see by the expressions on the faces of everyone in Security that they were delighted by these tiny travelers.

The kittens were loaded back into their carrier, and off they went to their gate. Kim called to let me know they had been assigned a seat, had their photos taken with the crew and pilots, and settled onto the plane.

The kittens traveled very well and napped in their carrier beneath the seat most of the flight. Midway through the trip, Kim took them into the bathroom and let them run around, stretch their legs, and have a little lunch.

They landed safely in Chicago, but the journey wasn't over. They still had another three-hour car ride ahead.

My folks met up with Kim and the kittens near the airline ticket counter. There were many hugs, smiles, thank-yous, and tears of joy. Then the kittens were turned over to my parents.

Once in the car, the kittens had a chance to use the litter box, have a little snack, and roam around for a bit. As soon as everyone was settled, they headed off to Iowa, with my dad as chauffeur and Mom in back with the babes.

THE KITTENS EVEN RECEIVED A CERTIFICATE FROM THE PILOT, COMMEMORATING THEIR FIRST FLIGHT.

It was a very long journey—nearly twelve hours from our house to my parents' house. The kittens did remarkably well—there wasn't a single glitch or problem along the way. Honestly, I couldn't imagine it going any better than it did.

The Frosts settled in quickly and are enjoying their life in Iowa. They spend a great part of each day watching wildlife out the window and are highly entertained by the birds, squirrels, and chipmunks that visit the feeders in my parents' backyard.

My parents are absolutely delighted by this pair of kittens, who bring a tremendous amount of joy into each day.

DEAR BUTTERBEAN,

I'm a tiny kitten, and sometimes when humans pick me up, I don't like it. I mean, I like being held, but sometimes the way they pick me up, especially the smaller humans, is a little uncomfortable and scary for me.

Can you please explain to all the big and small humans in the world how to properly pick up and hold a kitten?

Thanks,
Opal the Calico

**Dear Opal,**

It's a fact, humans like to pick up kittens. Kitties are floofy and soft, and I can understand the appeal, but I agree that humans should be educated!

Kittens are fragile things. Humans, please don't pick one up by the scruff of his neck, or by his legs, ears, or tail. This is a hard concept for younger humans to understand. A child might think of a kitten as a toy and not as a living thing.

To pick up a kitten, slide one hand underneath the kitten's chest, just behind the kitten's front legs. Gently lift the kitten and slide your other hand under the kitten's bottom and pull him toward your chest. If kitty seems uncomfortable, don't hold him tighter—instead, gently put him down. You don't want him to wriggle his way out of your arms, fall, and get injured.

You know what's better than picking up a kitten? Sitting quietly on the floor and letting the kitten come to you and climb into your lap!

I hope this helps, Tiny Tabby.

Be safe.

Love,
Charlene Butterbean

# Don't Fence Me In

Even when the kittens have full run of the house, there are times when I just don't want them underfoot. I use baby gates to section off areas. It gives them space to run, and it keeps them contained and out of my way.

This works for a while, but eventually they do realize they can climb to the top of the gate.

But when they get there, they don't know how to get back down, so they'll linger on top, pacing back and forth until they are rescued.

Yes, we rescue kittens in more ways than one.

# The No-Sew Cozy Kitty Bed

**H**ere's a kitty bed that's so simple to make, you can easily craft several and place one in each of kitty's napping spots. You can also make one to fit inside the kitty carrier. They're soft and super cozy, and they can protect the furniture from getting covered in cat hair.

## Here are the supplies you'll need:

- ½ yard of patterned fleece fabric
- ½ yard of solid-colored fleece fabric
- Yardstick or plastic ruler
- A pair of fabric scissors

1. Begin by cutting an 18" x 24" piece from each of your fabrics using a pair of fabric scissors.

2. Place the fabric rectangles together on a table and carefully line up all the sides. Smooth the fabric flat with your hand.

   Trim a 3" square from each of the four corners.

3. Cut 3" into the fleece layers at 1" intervals around all sides to create the "fringe."

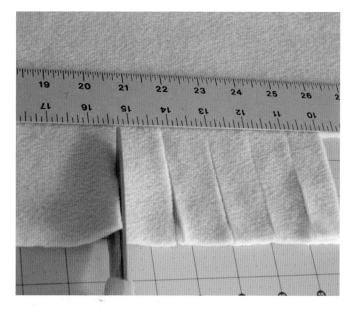

4. Take one piece of fringe from the top layer, and one from the bottom layer, and tie them together by making two knots.

5. Work your way around the entire blanket, knotting each pair of "fringe" together.

6. Place the completed fleece bed in a favorite napping spot for kitty to enjoy!

Meet The **MAGNIFICENT MEDLEY FAMILY**

During the winter months, we often have a break in fostering. It's not by choice—there just aren't a lot of kittens born that time of year, so there isn't much need for foster families.

We miss having kittens in the off-season, and the first batch that arrives after this break is always welcomed with a lot of excitement and enthusiasm.

It had been nearly two months since our last batch of kittens when the Magnificent Medley Family arrived.

Sometimes kittens are frightened of humans, and when they first move in, it can take awhile for them to get used to us. Sometimes kittens move into our house and act as though they've lived there their whole lives.

With the Medleys, they settled in and just made themselves right at home. It's always nice to have kittens be so sweet from the start.

Linus was a gentle, loving, clumsy cloud of a kitten— nearly all white, with two black smudges on his head.

When you have the looks of Linus Medley, everything you do is cute. Walking, running, sitting, blinking, sneezing, you name it, it's cute. Cute. Cute. Cute.

Peter looked like a tiny white panther, which earned him the nickname "Peter Panther." He had a squeaky mew, so we called him "Squeaky Pete" too. And we also called him "Peter Pants," just because it's funny to say.

*Freddie Jean*

*Kirby Nesbitt*

Kirby Nesbitt was a tiny orange guy. He had thin stripes around his belly, arms, and legs. His best friend in the bunch was his sister Freddie Jean, a tabby and tortie mix. They were quite close, and we were so happy when they were adopted together.

Beezus was a fuzzy tortie kitten filled with spunk and charm. Her wispy coat was nearly solid black in some parts and striped orange in others. She adored Charlene and was always snuggling up to her in hopes of getting a good bath.

*Beezus*

Maxine was a dark tabby with lovely stripes on her backside and dots on her belly. She was a bright and social girl, and an enchanting beauty too.

Maxine

All precious, and so varied in colors and personalities, these Medleys were a wonderful mix. We've had the pleasure of meeting several of them again as adult cats, and they're still very sweet, just like they were when we first met them.

Expressive
Kittens

# Kitten Communication

The first sounds kittens ever make are calls of distress—they cry out when they're in need of attention or food, or if they stray from their mom or family and feel lost.

- **Kittens use their tails to communicate.** A tail straight up means kitty is happy; if it's swishing back and forth, he could be plotting his next move or getting ready to pounce. A twitching tail can mean kitty is annoyed. Kittens puff out their tails and arch their backs when startled. This gesture is often accompanied by a hiss or growl. An anxious or nervous kitten will hold his tail low or tuck it between his legs.

- **Kittens will give you a little head butt to communicate that they like you.** They have scent glands on their foreheads, so when they brush against you, they are claiming you as their own by marking you with their scent. This scent is nothing a human can smell—just cats.

- **As they get older, kittens' vocabularies grow.** They will develop different types of meows to say "hello," "play with me," "let me in," "let me out," or "have you seen my sparkle ball?" If you pay close attention to your kitty, you can learn what each of these sounds means.

# Gordon Draper: Saddest Kitten in the World

# KITTY COMICS

## Charlene Doesn't Like to Share

Extreme
Naughtiness

# Kitten-Proofing

Before bringing home your new kitten, spend some time making your home a safe place for the wee one. Make sure an adult helps!

- **Small toy parts, buttons, coins, jewelry, thumbtacks, pins, ribbons, string, and rubber bands are all dangerous for kittens if consumed.** Anything small enough for a kitten to pick up in his mouth can cause choking or intestinal problems if swallowed. Pick up these small, dangerous objects and put them in a container or drawer.

- **Get in the habit of always keeping the toilet seat down.** You don't want a kitten falling in!

- **Move houseplants to higher ground**—many houseplants are poisonous to cats.

- **Move fragile and breakable items** out of kitty's reach.

- **Make sure windowscreens are secure** so kitty can't escape.

- **Move drapery and blind cords out of kitty's reach.**

- **Cover electrical cords and phone cords with plastic cord covers** to prevent kitty from chewing on them.

- **Make sure bathroom wastebaskets have lids** so kitty can't fish dangerous items like cotton balls or dental floss out.

**DEAR BUTTERBEAN,**

Can you please settle an argument between my brother and me? He says it's better to hide inside or under something—like in a box or under the bed. I say it's better to hide somewhere high—like on the back of the couch or on top of the kitty tower. Tell me, please, who is right.

I appreciate your time and expertise.

Your fan,
JIMMY TIPTON

### Dear Jimmy,

Well, you're both correct. Some cats feel safe and secure up high where they're able to survey the world below. Other cats prefer hiding on lower ground and like tucking themselves under things or into hidey-holes, because that makes them feel more comfortable. It's really about personal preference.

I go both ways—it all depends on my mood that day.

I hope this settles your little kitty fight.

Yours,
Charlene Butterbean

**DEAR BUTTERBEAN,**
EVERY DAY WHEN I WAKE UP, MY FIRST THOUGHT IS "WHAT SHALL I CLIMB TODAY?" IS THIS NORMAL? DO ALL KITTENS HAVE SUCH A DESIRE TO CLIMB?
THANKS,
OLIVER "ALL-OVER" FURMAN

**DEAR BUTTERBEAN,**
MY SEVERE CLIMBING HABIT HAS REACHED A NEW HIGH, AND NOW I'M GETTING MYSELF INTO TROUBLE. I KEEP GETTING INTO PLACES I CAN'T GET DOWN FROM.
WHAT SHOULD I DO?
ANONYMOUS

## Dear Oliver,

This urge to climb is completely natural for a kitten. Don't fight it, but please climb carefully.

Stay off the drapes—you could pull them down, anger your parents, and maybe injure yourself. Don't climb humans either. It's cute when you weigh a couple of pounds, but as you grow, it will become more painful for them.

Please stick to towers and posts designed especially for cats and kittens.

Be safe.

Love,
Charlene Butterbean

## Dear "Anonymous,"

STOP DOING IT. And have your parents block access to these dangerous places.

Love,
Charlene Butterbean

# Kittens of Mass Destruction

**I** heard an unusual rustling coming from the kitten room. I went in to investigate and discovered quite a scene—a whole litter of misbehaving kittens.

I had left their kitten climber a little too close to the table that held the tiny IBKC fund-raising telethon set, and the Suprenant Sisters had climbed up on the table and were engaged in acts of destruction and kitten merriment.

The tiny chairs were turned over; signs and numbers were on the ground and covered in tiny teeth marks. Kitten-sized telephones and coffee mugs were spilled all over the floor.

Betty June was hiding behind the curtain and batting at Biscuit, who was hanging on the other side, nearly pulling the curtains down. Marie-Noir was teething on the leg of a chair.

Everything was askew.

I think I got there just in the nick of time—it seemed it would be only a matter of moments before the walls started falling down.

A small team of kittens can do an incredible amount of damage in just a little bit of time when left unsupervised.

# Thurston Easterbrook
## Does His Very Best
## Michael Jackson Impersonation

And the white glove makes it quite convincing. He's the "Kitten King of Pop."

## Monroe Trimble

When we first met **Monroe Trimble**, he was a terribly shy kitten. He spent his early days with us hiding behind furniture and doors or tucked into corners. We barely saw more than the tip of his tail or the end of his whiskers. His brother and sister, Willard and Bess, were shy too, but not as shy as dear Monroe.

After some time, with great patience and the aid of some kitty treats, we were able to encourage him to step out into the world. We started to gain his trust, he let us pet him, and eventually he felt safe enough to climb into our laps. He enjoyed our affection, and finally he decided to start purring. He made great progress, but still, any sudden movement or noise would easily frighten him and send him scurrying away.

I wrote a long post on the blog about Monroe, describing his personality in detail, with hopes of attracting a patient and calm family to adopt him.

The next day, Emily e-mailed expressing an interest in adopting Monroe and one of his siblings too. She told me about the life she and her husband, Ty, lived. They were quiet people who enjoyed spending evenings together at home reading books and watching movies. They had lived with special-needs kittens before, so the challenges of a very shy kitten like Monroe didn't worry them at all.

They sounded perfect.

Monroe's siblings had already found their family, but I knew of a spunky and adorable foster kitten named Fisher, who looked an awful lot like Monroe. She was under the care of our friend Sue. I told Emily about Fisher, and she was excited to meet her too, so we made a date to introduce both kittens to their potential family.

When Emily, Ty, Sue, and Fisher arrived for our meeting, Monroe dashed into the bedroom to hide. That was fine, it gave Fisher a chance to say hello to everyone and it gave us all an opportunity to talk.

I went into the bedroom to check on Monroe. He had fallen asleep on top of the bed, making it easy for me to scoop him up and bring him back to the living room. I held him, and although his eyes were big and he was a wee bit scared, Emily and Ty got to see him up close and give him a few pats on the head and scratches on the chin.

A quick peek at this boy was all they needed. They decided they wanted to adopt the pair.

Monroe settled into his new home even faster than any of us expected. Emily reported that he spent the first day hiding under the bed, but by day two, with some encouragement from his little sister, he was out and about, and chasing her. He was even purring and licking the noses of his new family.

With the help of this patient family, sweet Monroe became a confident kitten. He felt safe; he felt loved. This was the perfect home for Monroe.

A MONTH LATER, HE WAS NEARLY COMPLETELY OVER HIS SHYNESS.

Kittens Grooming

# Bath Time for Bernadette

Poor little Bernadette Mayfield was looking a tad crusty and was in serious need of a bath.

So, into the sink she went, and what a good little girl she was. She didn't make a single peep the whole time she was in the water—she just waited patiently while she got a thorough but gentle bath.

Next, a good rinse followed by a towel dry.

Finally, a hair dryer was set on the quietest setting to take away all the dampness. She loved the warm air blowing on her belly.

After it was all over, she was tucked into her preheated bed and went straight to sleep.

All of her siblings got a bath too, but they all wiggled and cried through the whole process.

Bernadette means "brave little bear."
How fitting. That's exactly what she was.

# Dear Butterbean

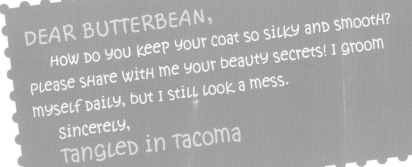

**DEAR BUTTERBEAN,**

HOW DO YOU KEEP YOUR COAT SO SILKY AND SMOOTH? PLEASE SHARE WITH ME YOUR BEAUTY SECRETS! I GROOM MYSELF DAILY, BUT I STILL LOOK A MESS.

SINCERELY,
**TANGLED IN TACOMA**

## Dear Tangled,

I was blessed with a coat that's naturally very glossy and requires hardly any brushing at all. I know most cats aren't so lucky. I recommend letting your humans brush you at least once a week. This will help remove dirt, keep your coat tangle free, and prevent you from getting hair balls.

I know at first it's kind of weird to be brushed, but you'll get used to it. Even if they touch that very sensitive spot on your belly, please don't bite or scratch them— they're doing it to help you.

Eating a healthy diet and drinking lots of water helps too.

Happy grooming,
Charlene Butterbean

Dear Clement,

You are not alone, Clement. Like trips to the vet, vacuum cleaners, and toddlers—nail trimmings are just one of those things most cats fear.

But it's important to keep your nails short. It protects you, your humans, their furniture and curtains, and keeps you out of trouble.

Please let them do it about every three weeks. It doesn't hurt, and it's for the best.

Hang in there,

Love,
Charlene Butterbean

# KITTY COMICS

## The Stare Down

## Maddie Bouvier

Alicia, a faithful follower of the IBKC, *adores* tortie kittens, so when we first introduced **Maddie Bouvier** on the blog, Alicia instantly fell in love. All tortie kittens are quite cute, but a little peach spot shaped like a tiny pair of lips on Maddie's nose made her an extra-special one.

We had an e-mail exchange about what an awesome little kitty Maddie was, and Alicia told me if there weren't thousands of miles between the two of them, she would have claimed this kitten.

Days later, I got an e-mail from Alicia's mom, Marion. She said it was Alicia's heart's desire to adopt Maddie, and she wondered if there was any way we could make this happen.

Normally, we don't like to adopt out our kittens without meeting the families first, but Alicia's mom was so sweet and kind, and the fact that she wanted to go these extra miles to fulfill her daughter's dream said so much about the kind of folks they were. They sounded like good, good people.

So, a plan was hatched.

As soon as Maddie was ready to go, Dennis, Alicia's dad, would fly all the way from Texas to pick up Maddie, and then deliver the most wonderful Christmas present ever to his daughter.

Maddie's bags were packed and we headed to the airport. We met Dennis near the ticket counter—he was easy to spot because he was carrying a bright red kitten carrier trimmed with white fur. The carrier was filled with everything a kitten would need to travel comfortably—a sporty red harness and leash, toys, treats, food, and water.

We sat down for a few minutes, filled out all the adoption paperwork, and chatted. Dennis had many questions and wanted to do everything he could to make sure Maddie had a safe and comfortable trip home. While we took care of business, Maddie was so patient, and even though it was a little noisy and chaotic at the airport on this Saturday afternoon, she curled up in our arms and stayed quiet and calm.

We said good-byes and Dennis headed to the ticket counter to show off Maddie to the agents. They were so enchanted by this girl and happy for her future that they upgraded their seats to first class!

At three a.m., I received an e-mail from a very shocked and excited Alicia, who could hardly believe that this dear sweet tortie Maddie, her dream kitty, was in her arms.

Maddie is five years old now and lives in Boston with Alicia, Alicia's husband, Tony, two more torties, and a dog! Even though she lives farther away from us than any of the other Itty Bitty Kitties, we're still in close contact with her, and we always get lots of Maddie reports from Alicia.

Maddie has grown up to be a beautiful, loving cat and still has a little peach mark shaped like a pair of lips on her nose.

SHE'S A HAPPY GIRL, WHO IS LOVED DEARLY.

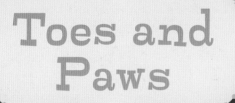
Toes and Paws

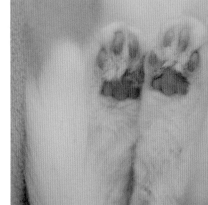

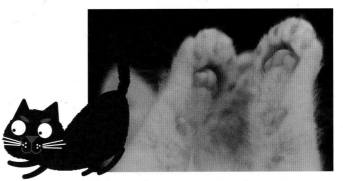

# Toes and Paws

Typically, a kitten has eighteen toes—five on each front paw and four on each back paw. The extra toe on each front paw is called a "dewclaw," and it's positioned like a thumb.

- **Cats with more than eighteen toes are called "polydactyl."**
  The world-record-holding kitten was born with twenty-eight toes!

- **Kitten paws sweat!** If a kitty gets too hot, she'll leave a damp trail of paw prints.

- **Kittens have to scratch!** It helps remove the dead outer layer of their nails, and it's their way of marking their territory. Because of this need, it's important to have a scratching post or pad available to them; otherwise, they may have no other option than to use the furniture or carpet.

- **A kitten's nails should be trimmed every few weeks (by an adult).**
  This protects him, the family, and the furniture!

# Cardboard Kitty Playhouse

It's a fact—cats love cardboard. Place a box on the floor, and most kitties will immediately climb inside to investigate. You can take take it a step further, by adding doors and windows, and make it a kitty playhouse!

To make your kitty playhouse, you will need the following items:

- A large, plain cardboard box
- Clear packing tape
- Markers
- A box cutter or serrated knife
  (and an adult to use it)

1. Tape your box closed with clear packing tape.

2. Use the markers to draw a front and back door, and several windows on your house. Make sure they're large enough for your kitty to pass through.

3. Use your imagination to decorate kitty's home. Draw shutters on the windows, add some window boxes, flowers, and shrubs on all sides of the house. Make it bright and fun!

4. Have an adult use a box cutter or knife to carefully cut out the windows and doors.

5. Toss a few toys inside the playhouse for kitty to enjoy!

Do you have more than one cat? Then create a whole cardboard kitty city for everyone! Or get fancy and make your playhouse a two-story by taping a second box on top!

Meet
The
SMALLS

**T**he Smalls spent their first couple of months in another foster home, along with their mama, Ruth. Ruth was a very young mom, just a tiny thing herself, and unable to produce enough milk to keep the kittens' bellies full and their bodies growing. The whole Small family was returned to the shelter to spend a little time with the doctors and staff, so they could get a little better and a lot bigger.

After a couple of weeks there, the kittens put on some weight and were released into our care. Mama Ruth stayed at the shelter, and once she was available for adoption, she quickly found a home.

The Small kittens still had lots of growing to do, especially **Louie**, the scrawniest of all the Smalls. Because of his tininess, he was given the nickname "Shrimp Louie."

Louie's toes were always cold, so he was constantly on a quest to find a place to warm them. A single sibling would do, but being in the middle of a pile of four kittens or snuggled up in the lap of a human was always better. He was a Flame Point Siamese, with bright blue eyes and a thin orange-striped tail. At first, his ears were huge compared to the rest of his parts, but as he got bigger, he grew into them.

**Violet Small**, the only girl in the group, was a Tortie Point Siamese with a freckled face and speckled toes. She was very affectionate and loved cuddling close to our faces. She would wrap her body and tail around our necks like a soft, purring scarf.

**Liam**, a handsome Lynx Point Siamese, was the biggest Small. His silver coat was silky, his eyes were deep and blue, and his nose was a perfect pink triangle.

**Solomon Small** was a chatty Seal Point Siamese with a chocolate-brown face and a toasted almond coat. Sometimes we called him Sol, but more often we called him "Monkey." He always loved climbing and leaping, and he could easily scale the curtains or any piece of furniture. When I prepared the Smalls' meals, Sol would always climb up my back and balance on my shoulders while I loaded their plate, rinsed the cat food can, and carried the meal into their room. As I leaned over to place the plate on the floor, he would jump from my back and land with a thud. This sound was a signal to the others that it was time to eat, and they would all come running.

Solomon

The Smalls were very beautiful and wonderful, each in their own way, but what made this batch of kittens extra-special was their sweetness. From the day they moved in, they were so warm and loving to each other and to any person they met. We had lots of visitors during their stay with us, and everyone was charmed and dazzled by this litter of kittens.

All the kittens found fabulous homes. Violet and Liam were adopted together, and Louie and Sol left separately, but moved into homes with other young cats. Each of them is happy, healthy, and much larger now.

Belly Stripes
and Spots

# A Few Feeding Tips

Be sure you feed your kitten a food that's specifically for kitties and not for adult cats. Kittens grow fast, use lots of energy, and have different nutritional needs than big cats do.

- **Kittens have tiny stomachs, so it's difficult to give them all the calories they need in just one or two meals.** Three or four small meals are best to start, and as the kitten grows, this can be reduced to fewer, but larger, meals. We feed our kitties a combination of wet and dry food. Wet at mealtime, and dry is always available to them for grazing and snacking. Your vet can help determine the food and the frequency that is best for each stage of your kitty's development.

- **Kitten food is much higher in calories than adult food, so if you have adult cats in your house, be sure to keep them away from it.** Too much nibbling on the kitten kibble can quickly lead to overweight cats.

- **To keep your big cat out of the little kitty's food, take a cardboard box,** cut a hole big enough for kitty but too small for the adult cat to pass through, and place the kitty food inside.

- **Keep the bowls clean and change the water at least once a day.**

- **Ceramic or stainless steel bowls are better than plastic dishes.** Plastic dishes are easy to spill, which kittens will do, and also harder to keep clean. They get scratched, and harmful bacteria can grow in these scratches.

Norman
Ashby,
You're
Doing It
Wrong

# Graham Loudermilk

**A**ll of the Loudermilks except **Graham** had found their homes and were starting to leave our nest. Graham was big, he was ready, and it was time for him to start the next chapter in his life. I sent a message out to all of our friends to see if any of them might need a kitten to add to their world.

Our friend and neighbor Briana was very curious about this handsome buff-colored boy, and wondered if Graham could come by for a visit and meet their big tabby love, Melvin.

Briana and her family had been visiting shelters, and they had met with a few cats, hoping to find one that might get along nicely with Melvin. A few had sparked their interest, but they weren't quite ready to commit to any one of those cats yet.

I packed up Graham in the carrier and walked over to their house. Briana met me at the door with a huge smile, and I came in and placed the carrier on the floor. Melvin woke from his nap on the couch, and hopped down to investigate.

Noses bumped, paws reached, both were curious and calm.

We waited a few moments, then I opened the carrier door, and Graham eased his way out. Melvin stayed close.

Not a single growl was growled or hiss was hissed. Never in a squillion years did I think the first few moments would go as great as this.

The boys continued to check each other out as Graham explored the room, the whole first floor of the house, and then made his way upstairs. Melvin followed close, and so did we.

It was clear things were going well. It seemed Graham might just be the perfect little brother for Melvin, so it was decided, this would be Graham's new home. He would be a very special Christmas surprise for the rest of the family.

We wanted the timing to be perfect, so we waited for the next evening that was free of appointments, commitments, and lessons to deliver this precious present.

I found a box lid that was slightly larger than the kitty carrier and wrapped all but one side of it with Christmas paper, then trimmed it with a bow. I placed Graham in the carrier, slid the carrier into the box, and then

Craig and I walked over to Briana's house with the surprise in hand.

The kids were at the table finishing their dinner when we arrived. I placed the package on the floor with the open side of the box concealed, and announced that we were here to deliver a special Christmas gift for the family.

The kids came closer and Graham let out a few mews. Mouths dropped

open, eyes got big, and Caleb, their son, screamed "O . . . M . . . G" and threw his arms in the air. We slid the carrier out of the box and released little Graham to say hello to the whole family.

As you can imagine, Caleb, Yahbi, and Sega were shocked, surprised, and thrilled by this gift. Smiles were huge and abundant, hearts were happy.

The kids were so sweet. They took turns holding Graham and playing with him and even in all the excitement of getting a new kitten, they didn't forget about Melvin, who could easily have been overlooked. They gave him lots of love too.

Craig and I stayed for a bit and enjoyed talking with the family and soaking in this lovely scene. The kids, again and again, thanked us for their kitten.

It took a while for Graham to find his home, but he found his perfect family and they were worth the wait!

THEY WERE ALL IN AWE OF HIS TININESS AND ADORABLENESS.

# A Message from Astrid

I left my computer for just one moment to go check on a noise I heard coming from the other room. I returned to find that Astrid Easterbrook had typed a little message on my keyboard.

Here is what she had to say . . .

I'm not sure exactly what it means, but I'm guessing what she was trying to say was "purrrrrrrr," because that's what Astrid Easterbrook says *all* the time.

# Dear Butterbean

DEAR BUTTERBEAN,

I am a recently adopted three-month-old kitty. My new sister is a fourteen-year-old tabby, and I don't think she likes me one bit.

I've tried everything to win her over. I chase her, bat at her swishing tail, and pounce on her when she's not expecting it. These things—which are so fun for me—seem to anger her.

Am I doing something wrong?

TROUBLED TORTIE TODDLER

## Dear Troubled Tortie Toddler,

Your behavior is completely normal for a kitten of your age, but it's no fun for a fourteen-year-old cat.

Think about things *she* might like to do. Do you share a common interest, like eating, perhaps? Maybe you can share a meal together—that could be pleasant for both of you, and maybe a good way for you to bond.

Hold off on the chasing and pouncing for a while. She may warm up to the idea eventually, but for now, take it easy and give her some time and space to adjust to this new change in her life.

Yours truly,
Charlene Butterbean

DEAR BUTTERBEAN,

I am a fourteen-year-old tabby and recently my family adopted a three-month-old tortie kitten.

Since the kitten arrived, I have been completely on edge. I am constantly being chased or pounced upon. She's invaded my most sacred napping spaces, and I feel like all my humans are ignoring me and giving her all the attention.

I don't like it. Nope. Not one little bit.

TROUBLED TABBY SENIOR

Dear Troubled Tabby Senior,

I'm sure this adjustment has been very difficult for you. You've had the house and your humans all to yourself for a long time, and now you're forced to share.

I think it's important for you to speak up and let the family know that you're missing their attention. Now, don't go doing something rash like pooping on someone's pillow. Just give them a few extra head butts to let them know you love and need them.

Or maybe try joining in on some kitten fun. Remember how you used to love chasing Ping-Pong balls across the hardwood floors? Maybe give it a try with the kitten.

Perhaps you'll find that having a kitten around isn't such a bad thing after all.

Yours truly,
Charlene Butterbean

Charlene and Friends

# Games for Kittens

## Fishing for Prizes

Collect a minimum of ten paper towel tubes and glue them together to form a pyramid. Once the glue has dried, toss a few sparkle balls and furry mice, and sprinkle a few kitty treats inside the tubes.

Your kitten will have a great time peeking inside and using her paws to fish the toys and treats out of them. Once she grabs them all, refill the tubes and play again.

# Kitten Agility Course

**P**ull out kitty's scratching posts, tunnels, kitten climbers, and a few boxes. Line them up in a row and create a little agility course.

Use a feather wand to encourage her to run the course: scale each tower, climb over every box, and go through each tunnel. Reward her with a treat when she finishes.

Do you have two kittens? Time them and see who gets through the course the fastest!

## Laundry Basket Busy Box

Stuff some soft toys into the holes of a laundry basket, and twist on a few pipe cleaners and zip ties too. Put kitty inside the Laundry Basket Busy Box, and let her pull the toys out, fiddle with the pipe cleaners and zip ties, and wrestle around inside the basket.

It's a great way to keep her entertained, engaged, and out of trouble for a little bit.

# KITTY COMICS

## Home-Schooled Kitten

High-Fiving Kittens

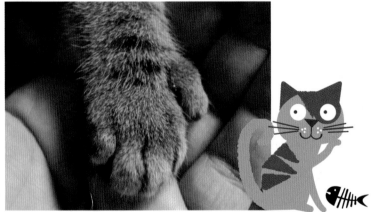

# Tips on Taking Better Kitten Pictures

- **Timing Is Everything.** The best time to take a photo of a kitten is when he's starting to wind down or just waking up. If you try to take photos while a kitten is active and in the middle of playtime, most likely the images will be blurry.

- **Lots of Light.** Turn off the flash on your camera and photograph the kitten in a room that has lots of windows and natural light. When you use a flash on your camera, especially when you're very close to the kitten, it will cause "red eye," and his eyes will appear red in the photograph. Also, the brightness of the flash can be unpleasant and startling to a kitten.

- **Tidy Up.** Make sure the background is clutter free, and try to photograph the kitten in a nice, clean setting.

- **Get Down on Their Level.** Instead of looking down on the kitten from above, get down on the same level to take a photograph.

- **Grab Their Attention.** Crinkle a foil ball, rattle a toy, or make a sound to get their attention. If you can't do this and hold on to your camera too, get someone to help you. You can also get their attention by wiggling a toy in front of them, but sounds work better. Some toys can get the kittens too excited and they'll move too much, making it more difficult to photograph them.

- **Take a Lot of Pictures.** Take a lot of pictures, delete the blurry or bad ones, and keep the good ones.

## While you were sleeping . . .

I stuck my paw in your bedside water glass.

Then I sat on your chest and watched you sleep with your mouth wide open.

I followed Drewey downstairs and sat by her while she had a snack in the kitchen.

I stared out the front window but nothing was happening outside.

So I took a bath on the dining room table.

And I ordered a heated pet bed from an infomercial on television and paid for it using your credit card. (Just three easy payments of $49.99, and if I'm not fully satisfied I can return it.)

I chewed on your earbuds. It's not my fault, you left them out!

Then I jumped up on the bed, tiptoed across the pillows, curled up next to you, and started purring.

"Good kitten," you said.

Hiding,
Lurking,
Perching

Against the Day

THOMAS PYNCHON

BAZAAR STYLE  Selina Lake and Joanna Simmons

Indian Interiors

By Hand

Paris Interiors

Annette Messager   WORD FOR WORD

AT HOME WITH pattern

PUNYA

# Litter Box Tips

Using the litter box is instinctive, so for most kittens, no training is required.

- **Keep the litter box in a location that's convenient for the kitten.**
  Kitty likes a little privacy, but don't try to hide the box so it's difficult for kitty to find.

- **Sometimes accidents happen, and kitty might stop using the box. This can happen for many reasons:**
  It could be a medical issue.
  She doesn't like the type of box or location of it.
  She doesn't like the type of litter, or there's too much or not enough of it in the box.
  She doesn't like sharing the box with the other cats.

- **Make sure it's kitten-sized and not too tall for kitty to climb into.**
  Upgrade the litter box as the kitty grows.

- **Don't place the litter box too close to kitty's food and water dishes.**
  If it's too close, it's easy for the kitten to kick the litter into the dishes and consume the litter.

- **Keep it clean!** Kittens and cats can be very fussy about the cleanliness of their boxes. A litter box should be scooped (at least) daily. Once a week, the box should be dumped and cleaned, and the litter should be replaced.

- **If you have multiple cats,** it's good to have one more box than the number of cats in your home.

# Clovis and Rupert Ashby

In the past, animals had always found their way to Kendra. She had never been in the position of being able to "pick" her own pet. So, on the day she visited all the Itty Bitty Kitties, she was feeling a tad overwhelmed by this task. Excited, but overwhelmed.

After spending some time with the kittens and getting to know them a bit, **Rupert Ashby** was the one she chose. He was especially dazzling that day, so we weren't surprised at all that he was the one she picked.

Rupert wasn't quite ready to leave our home—he had a few ounces to gain before he was big enough to be adopted.

Kendra couldn't wait until adoption day to see her boy again, so she came back for a visit. When she arrived, Rupert was asleep in the kitten basket and **Clovis** was next to him, fully alert, and completely charming.

He just wiggled and squiggled around in there, offering his paws to Kendra,

**HE WAS COMPLETELY IRRESISTIBLE.**

batting his eyelashes, and showing her his round little belly.

She didn't have much of a visit with Rupert, but she sure had a great time with Clovis.

The next day, Kendra called to tell me that Clovis had stolen her heart, and she wanted to adopt him too!

We were thrilled by this news—we always prefer sending kittens out in pairs whenever possible, and these two made such an adorable set!

They all live just a few blocks away from us, and whenever we bump into Kendra, she always tells us how grateful she is for them both.

# Two Kittens Are Better Than One

When we adopt our kittens out, we always prefer for them to go with one of their siblings, or to a home with another kitten or young cat. Here are a few reasons why two kitties can be better than just one.

- **Without a companion to keep him occupied,** a single kitten can find all sorts of trouble to get into, and he can be more destructive.

- **In order to develop socially,** kittens need to interact with other kittens.

- **No kitten likes being lonely.** We humans can offer some company, but we're not as much fun as another kitten, no matter how hard we try.

- **It's really fun watching two kittens play.** *Really* fun!

- **Kittens can learn a lot from each other.** If there is a skill one is lacking, he can pick it up from his sibling.

# A Crossword with Kenneth Wiggins

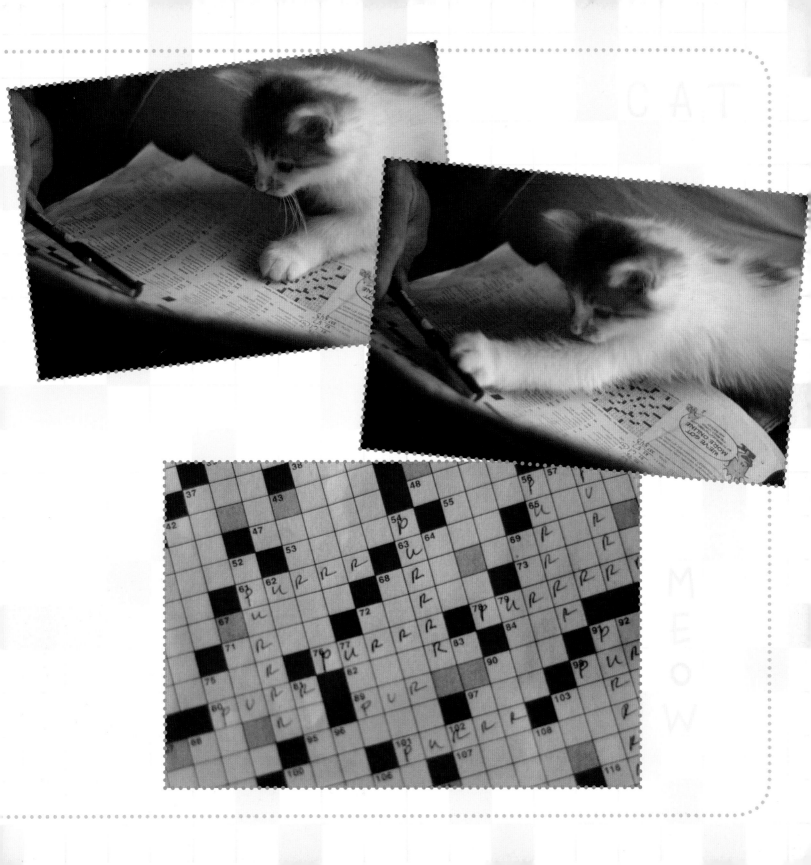

Meet
# The DEARBORNS

I got a call from the Foster Department announcing that a new set of kittens had arrived. The babies sounded adorable—they were a nice mix of colors and coat lengths. We always enjoy variety! I was anxious to meet them, so I set up their quarters and dashed to the shelter to pick them up.

They were even cuter than described! Each tiny kitten was completely unique. There was Pearla, a soft gray and white kitten with dark eyes and a pink button nose; Sheldon, a Siamese with the grumpiest expression on his face; Marla, a gorgeous calico girl; and Geraldine, a goofy, long-haired girl with a floofy coat and a loud voice. Because they were so sweet from the start, they were given the last name "Dearborn."

Pearla

Later that afternoon I received a second phone call. Another Dearborn had arrived at the shelter!

A fifth kitten in this litter?

Well, as it turns out the gentleman who had brought the four Dearborns into the shelter that morning had returned with one more.

Early that morning, he had discovered the first four kittens in the wall of an old garage. Later that afternoon, he checked the wall once more to be sure he had collected all the kittens, and he found kitten number five! He returned to the shelter with her so she could be reunited with her family. The poor little thing was covered in dirt and dust, and was dehydrated too.

Sheldon

Phoebe

Back to the shelter I went, and there she was— Phoebe Dearborn, all by herself in a cubby in the foster room, screaming at the top of her little lungs.

I boxed her up and headed home with her—the poor little girl cried nearly the whole way!

When we arrived, I put Phoebe in the kitten kennel with her siblings. I thought they might be a little more excited to see her, but they just went about their business. No big, grand hellos, more of an "oh, there you are, why didn't you come with us before" kind of greeting.

We are so grateful that the kind gentleman went looking for Phoebe! She completed this perfect set of mismatched kittens.

Marla

Geraldine

Hugging
Kittens

# Wylla Stout

**W**ylla **Stout** was a ridiculously cute kitten. Her body was tiny, but her gorgeous, untamed, multi-colored coat was gigantic— it looked nearly three sizes too large for her! From this floofy parka, two tiny triangle ears protruded and two perfectly round eyes peered out. She had all the right parts in all the right places, but the size of each piece was a wee bit off—a little too big or a little too small—which made her look a little bit odd. Adorable, but odd.

Shortly after Wylla arrived, we noticed that she was having problems digesting her food. She was a very good eater, and would consume anything we put in front of her, but most of what she swallowed came back up. After many visits to the vet and lots of tests and X-rays, Wylla was diagnosed with a rare condition called Megaesophagus.

With this condition, Wylla's body wasn't able to properly move the food into her stomach, and it would just sit in her esophagus (the tube that connects her throat to her stomach). Eventually, she would throw most of it back up.

There's nothing doctors can do to correct Megaesophagus, no surgeries or procedures can improve it, so we had to learn how to help her manage it so she could keep the food down, and get the nutrition she needed to grow.

Our doctor suggested trying small, frequent meals instead of fewer, larger

ones. Her food needed to be blended smooth, and instead of placing her food dish on the floor, we needed to elevate it, and try training her to eat standing upright. With her body stretched out, gravity would help pull the food into her stomach. The vet also suggested that after each meal we hold her upright for several minutes, to help the food continue to pass.

We took his advice, and with much trial and error, figured out what worked best for Wylla. She started getting a little bit bigger, much healthier, and closer to an "adoptable" state.

It was then that we decided that, after all we had been through with this dear little girl, there was no way we could possibly let her leave our nest—so we adopted Wylla Stout ourselves!

She's a special one—so sweet, cuddly and affectionate, very chatty and full of character and life. Charlene adores her and loves having Wylla as a playmate, napping partner, and friend.

On occasion, Wylla still struggles with her medical condition, but she has far more good days than bad days now. She's more work than the average kitten, but she's worth it!

Meet
The
ANDERSON-ERICKSONS

**W**hen we first met the Anderson-Erickson kittens, they were dusty and dirty little things. We usually don't know where our kittens were before they came into the shelter, but I would guess this set was most likely living outside. They were a mess, and they were shy—it seemed like they hadn't been handled much at all by humans.

They all needed a bath immediately, so one by one, each kitten was pulled from the kitty carrier and cleaned up before getting placed in their room. It wasn't the best introduction to our home, but it had to be done!

Emory

There were six kittens in total—some were black with white, some were white with black. Several of them looked an awful lot alike, and it was really hard to tell them apart. As we got to know them, though, it became easier to figure out who was who.

Emory and Ferris were nearly identical twins. Both were tuxedos with white bibs and white toes. Their whiskers were long, white, and a little crinkly.

Bernice

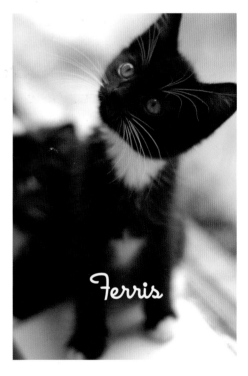
Ferris

Bernice was the quietest and shyest in the bunch. She was black with white, like Emory and Ferris. The tips of her toes on her right foot were white, but on the left front leg, she wore a tall white sock.

Ambrose was a tuxedo too, but his coat was much shaggier and longer than the other black with white kittens.

Clement, who was white with black spots, was the troublemaker in the bunch. He was a climber, and on many occasions, he had to be rescued from harm's way and removed from the drapes. He could climb up them, but never down again.

Last of all, there was Louise. She was white with black marks too, and it looked like she was wearing a little black wig with a part in the middle. She had a funny little smudge on her nose and chin.

At first, six kittens seem manageable, but as they grew bigger, it seemed they grew in numbers too. Everywhere we looked, there was an Anderson-Erickson!

When it was time to go, they all left in pairs—Ambrose with Louise, Clement with Bernice, and Emory with Ferris. Six kittens, three wonderful families.

At most animal shelters, you have to be at least sixteen years old to volunteer. Some shelters have a junior volunteer program for kids fourteen and up, and they are allowed to volunteer along with a parent. Even if you're not old enough to volunteer, that doesn't mean you can't help the animals out! Here are a few ways you can contribute and make a difference in the life of an animal.

## Have a Fundraiser for Your Local Animal Shelter

Two of our little friends, Opal and Lola, who were only five and six years old, set up a lemonade stand with the help of their parents. They donated all of their profits to our Humane Society and asked that the money be used specifically to help the kitties.

## Have a Pet-Food Drive

Most shelters are in need of food for the animals in their care and also for their food bank. The food bank helps supply poorer families in the community with food for their pets.

It's important to keep the food banks stocked, because when people can't afford to feed their pets, often their only option is to surrender their animals to the shelter. So, by helping the food bank, you're

helping families stay together with their pets and keeping the population lower at the shelter too.

A pet-food drive is easy to do. Just ask your friends, neighbors, and even local grocery stores or pets stores to donate cans of wet food or bags of dry food for the cause, and with the help of an adult, deliver them to the shelter.

## Collect Supplies

Bath towels, blankets, paper towels, newspaper, cat toys, cat beds, kitty litter, cleaning supplies, and laundry detergent are all things animal shelters use every day.

Collect a few of these items from your home, friends, and neighbors and donate them to your local shelter.

## Make Some Kitty Beds

Follow the instructions on pages 36–38 and make a few kitty beds for shelter cats. Every kitten and cat appreciates a cozy bed to sleep in!

## Foster a Kitten (or Litter)

The summer months are the busiest ones at animal shelters. Many orphaned kittens and kittens with mothers come into the shelters daily, and there isn't enough space to house them or staff to take care of everyone.

If your family has the time to commit to a foster kitten or litter, and the space in your home to do it, it's a wonderful way to help kittens out!

# Where Are They Meow?

**H**ere are a few of our itty bitty kitties—when they were wee and now, all grown up.

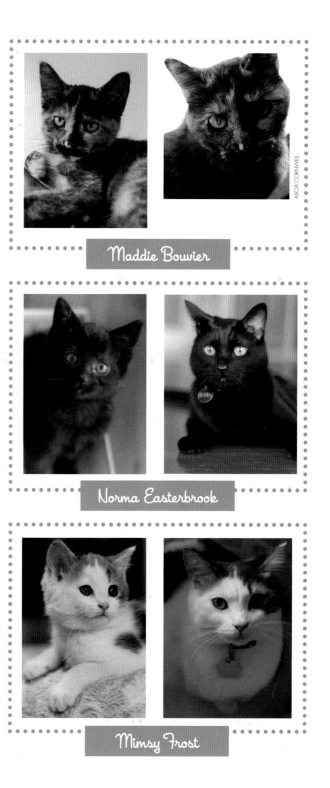

Maddie Bouvier

Norma Easterbrook

Mimsy Frost

Nigel Frost

Baxter Lamm

ALICIA CORNWELL

Phoebe Dearborn

Linus Medley

Thurston Easterbrook

Geraldine Dearborn

"Shrimp Louie" Small

Benny Musselman